Quilt ART 2010
ENGAGEMENT CALENDAR

A COLLECTION OF PRIZEWINNING
QUILTS FROM ACROSS THE COUNTRY

Quilts researched and selected by Klaudeen Hansen

Color photography by Charles R. Lynch, Paducah, KY

On the cover:
THE BLUE GOOSE
by Janet Blum, Sturgis, SD, 60" x 60". Janet chose Judy Niemeyer's pattern for her first quilt with curved piecing. Because of the circular design, her placement of cool colors was used to create motion. Machine quilted by Judy Woodworth, Gering, NE. Won the first-place ribbon at Black Hills Quilt Show, Rapid City, SD.

Features Autumn Splendor pattern by Judy Niemeyer Quilting, ©August 2006.

KT-22 IN CLOTH

by B. Lynn Tubbe, Georgetown, CA, 46" x 46". Adaptation of Cecile Johnson's noted *Squaw Valley* watercolor painting. This quilt uses only fabric and thread. The black diamond symbolized the challenges, both skiing and quilting, of this peak. Ribbon winner at Road to California, Ontario, CA; Pacific International Quilt Festival, Long Beach, CA; and juried into the AQS Quilt Show and Contest, Paducah, KY.

Adaptation of Cecile Johnson's Squaw Valley, ©1970 Laura Iwanski for Cecile Johnson

December/January

MONDAY
28

TUESDAY
29

WEDNESDAY
30

THURSDAY
31

FRIDAY
1   New Year's Day

SATURDAY
2

SUNDAY
3

JANUARY

S	M	T	W	T	F	S
					1	2
3	4	5	6	7	8	9
10	11	12	13	14	15	16
17	18	19	20	21	22	23
24	25	26	27	28	29	30
31						

PICCADILLY SQUARE

by Julie Gardner, Oxnard, CA, 84" x 84". The idea for this quilt came from *Kaffe Fassett's Quilt Road*. Machine-pieced borders added excitement to this piece. Machine quilted by Andrea Gillingham. Received Judges' Choice Award at Glendale Quilt Show, CA.

Features Postcard Quilt pattern, *Kaffe Fassett's Quilt Road*, Rowan Patchwork & Quilting designs, C&T Publishing, ©2005.

January

MONDAY
4

TUESDAY
5

WEDNESDAY
6

THURSDAY
7

FRIDAY
8

SATURDAY
9

SUNDAY
10

			JANUARY			
S	M	T	W	T	F	S
					1	2
3	4	5	6	7	8	9
10	11	12	13	14	15	16
17	18	19	20	21	22	23
24	25	26	27	28	29	30
31						

CROSSROADS & TRAFFIC CIRCLES

by Klaudeen Hansen, Sun Prairie, WI, 37" x 48". Working with the octagon shape brought Klaudeen to this original woven illusion and a great place to use her black-and-white fabric collection. Hand-quilted traffic circles embellish the primary colored squares and triangles. Premiere showings at St. Benedict Gallery, Madison, WI; and Prairie Heritage Quilt Show, Sun Prairie, WI.

January

MONDAY
11

TUESDAY
12

WEDNESDAY
13

THURSDAY
14

FRIDAY
15

SATURDAY
16

SUNDAY
17

			JANUARY			
S	M	T	W	T	F	S
					1	2
3	4	5	6	7	8	9
10	11	12	13	14	15	16
17	18	19	20	21	22	23
24	25	26	27	28	29	30
31						

A DIFFERENT DIRECTION

by Mary Kay Davis, Sunnyvale, CA, 60" x 60". The bright orange is a creative setting for a Mariner's Compass design by Judy Mathieson. Paper piecing, hand appliqué, and multicolored thread are featured with machine stipple quilting. Winner at the Denver National Quilt Festival, CO; and juried into AQS Quilt Expo, Nashville, TN.

Features a Mariner's Compass pattern by Judy Mathieson ©1994.

January

MONDAY
18 — Martin Luther King Jr. Day

TUESDAY
19

WEDNESDAY
20

THURSDAY
21

FRIDAY
22

SATURDAY
23

SUNDAY
24

JANUARY

S	M	T	W	T	F	S
					1	2
3	4	5	6	7	8	9
10	11	12	13	14	15	16
17	18	19	20	21	22	23
24	25	26	27	28	29	30
31						

COLORING AROUND AND AROUND

by JoAnn Belling, Des Moines, IA, 30" x 50". The colorwash technique illustrates color relations, intensity, values, contrasts and densities. Squares, rectangles, triangles, and diamonds add complexity to the fabric placement and construction. Machine-pieced and quilted. Displayed in several gallery and museum shows and the Iowa State Fair, Des Moines.

January

MONDAY
25

TUESDAY
26

WEDNESDAY
27

THURSDAY
28

FRIDAY
29

SATURDAY
30

SUNDAY
31

JANUARY

S	M	T	W	T	F	S
					1	2
3	4	5	6	7	8	9
10	11	12	13	14	15	16
17	18	19	20	21	22	23
24	25	26	27	28	29	30
31						

ABRAHAM LINCOLN'S QUILT

by Jenifer Dick, Harrisonville, MO, 90" x 90". Desiring to honor Abe Lincoln and her son named after Abe, Jenifer chose the Whig Rose for the center medallion because Lincoln was a Whig before he was a Republican. Steps to the White House blocks surround the center. Quilted by Don Sutcliffe of Peculiar, MO. First-place winner at Missouri State Fair; and juried into AQS Quilt Expo, Nashville, TN.

February

MONDAY
1

TUESDAY   *Groundhog Day*
2

WEDNESDAY
3

THURSDAY
4

FRIDAY
5

SATURDAY
6

SUNDAY
7

FEBRUARY

S	M	T	W	T	F	S
	1	2	3	4	5	6
7	8	9	10	11	12	13
14	15	16	17	18	19	20
21	22	23	24	25	26	27
28						

STRING OF PEARLS

by Mary S. Buvia, Greenwood, IN, 75" x 84". Original design inspired by symbols of love. Machine appliqué; couching; curved piecing; piping; and dimensional, turned-edge, and raw-edge appliqué are some of the many techniques. Honored with Best of Show at Indiana Heritage Quilt Show, Bloomington, IN; and Honorable Mention at AQS Quilt Show & Contest, Paducah, KY.

February

MONDAY
8

TUESDAY
9

WEDNESDAY
10

THURSDAY
11

FRIDAY
12

SATURDAY
13

SUNDAY
14

Valentine's Day

FEBRUARY

S	M	T	W	T	F	S
		1	2	3	4	5	6
7	8	9	10	11	12	13
14	15	16	17	18	19	20
21	22	23	24	25	26	27
28						

PEONIES FOR GRANDMA

by Sandi McMillan, Albion, NE, 79" x 79". This quilt began as a Broken Star but was scrapped due to a math error. Teaming up with Susan DuLaney's Peony-corner pattern helped Sandi complete this hand appliquéd and machine-quilted beauty. First-place winner at Nebraska State Fair, and displayed in her one woman special exhibit for AQS Quilt Expo, Des Moines, IA.

Features Peony-corner pattern by Susan DuLaney of Distinctive Pieces ©1994.

February

MONDAY
15 — Presidents' Day

TUESDAY
16

WEDNESDAY
17 — Ash Wednesday

THURSDAY
18

FRIDAY
19

SATURDAY
20

SUNDAY
21

FEBRUARY

S	M	T	W	T	F	S
		1	2	3	4	5	6
7	8	9	10	11	12	13
14	15	16	17	18	19	20
21	22	23	24	25	26	27
28						

CRYSTAL REVELATION

by Susan Nelson, Prior Lake, MN, 72" x 72". The dramatic jewel tones emphasize shapes that radiate from the center and resonate throughout this original design quilt. First-place winner Minnesota State Quilt Show, Rochester; and displayed at AQS Quilt Show & Contest, Paducah, KY.

February

MONDAY
22

TUESDAY
23

WEDNESDAY
24

THURSDAY
25

FRIDAY
26

SATURDAY
27

SUNDAY
28

FEBRUARY

S	M	T	W	T	F	S
		1	2	3	4	5	6
7	8	9	10	11	12	13
14	15	16	17	18	19	20
21	22	23	24	25	26	27
28						

DRAGONFLY DIAMONDS

by Kathy Timmons, Nashville, TN, 82" x 90". An Internet group challenge by Linda Franz to create blocks from her *Quilted Diamonds* books prompted Kathy to hand piece these 185 blocks. Diamond blocks "asked" Kathy to set them into a diamond medallion. Hand quilted by Lizzie Ann Mast. Juried into AQS Quilt Expo, Nashville, TN.

Features patterns from *Quilted Diamonds* and *Quilted Diamonds 2* by Linda Franz ©2002 & 2004.

March

MONDAY
1

TUESDAY
2

WEDNESDAY
3

THURSDAY
4

FRIDAY
5

SATURDAY
6

SUNDAY
7

MARCH

S	M	T	W	T	F	S
		1	2	3	4	5	6
7	8	9	10	11	12	13
14	15	16	17	18	19	20
21	22	23	24	25	26	27
28	29	30	31			

HAPPY, HAPPY, HAPPY

by Nancy Arseneault, Tucson, AZ, 76" x 76". Inspired by the Country Whig Rose pattern by Kim Diehl, Nancy used nine blocks, deconstructed them for the center, and added an original border. Invisible machine appliqué and machine quilting. Viewers' Choice winner at Quilt Fiesta! in Tucson.

Features Country Whig Rose pattern from *Simple Blessings* by Kim Diehl ©2004 Martingale & Co.

March

MONDAY
8

TUESDAY
9

WEDNESDAY
10

THURSDAY
11

FRIDAY
12

SATURDAY
13

SUNDAY
14

Daylight Saving Time begins

MARCH

S	M	T	W	T	F	S
		1	2	3	4	5	6
7	8	9	10	11	12	13
14	15	16	17	18	19	20
21	22	23	24	25	26	27
28	29	30	31			

CIRCLES OF FRIENDS

by Rebecca Polgar, Minong, WI; Gail Stepanek, Heather Rowswell, Melody Lenort, and Nancy Mancke, IL, 74" x 65". Five friends formed a group to challenge their quiltmaking skills. Pattern ideas inspired by Ring Around the Rosy by Dianne Hire and Beauty on the Nile by Claudia Clark Myers. Double ribbon winner at Minnesota Quilt Show, Rochester, MN.

Features Beauty on the Nile pattern by Claudia Clark Myers and pattern from *Quilters Playtime: Games with Fabric* by Dianne S. Hire, AQS, ©2004.

March

MONDAY
15

TUESDAY
16

WEDNESDAY   *St. Patrick's Day*
17

THURSDAY
18

FRIDAY
19

SATURDAY   *National Quilting Day*
20

SUNDAY
21

MARCH

S	M	T	W	T	F	S
	1	2	3	4	5	6
7	8	9	10	11	12	13
14	15	16	17	18	19	20
21	22	23	24	25	26	27
28	29	30	31			

VANISHING POINT

by Chris Lynn Kirsch, Watertown, WI, 50" x 50". Made for a guild's On Point challenge, the quilt was to look as if one square was turned on its point and placed on top of a second square. Foundation pieced, machine quilted. Juried into AQS Quilt Expo, Nashville, TN.

March

MONDAY
22

TUESDAY
23

WEDNESDAY
24

THURSDAY
25

FRIDAY
26

SATURDAY
27

SUNDAY
28

			MARCH			
S	M	T	W	T	F	S
		1	2	3	4	5	6
7	8	9	10	11	12	13
14	15	16	17	18	19	20
21	22	23	24	25	26	27
28	29	30	31			

MARINER'S COMPASS

by Pat Current, Apple Valley, MN, 95" x 95". Using M'Liss Rae Hawley's Mariner's Medallion, Pat intended to make a wallhanging using four compasses, but enjoyed making the units so much that she made a large quilt. The fun of collecting the fabrics kept her interest in high gear. Shown at Bag Lady Show in Eagan, MN; State Guild Show, Rochester, MN; and ribbon winner at the Minnesota State Fair, St. Paul.

Features patterns from *Mariner's Medallion Quilts* by M'Liss Rae Hawley, C&T Publishing, 2006.

March/April

MONDAY
29

TUESDAY
30   Passover

WEDNESDAY
31

THURSDAY
1   April Fools' Day

FRIDAY
2   Good Friday

SATURDAY
3

SUNDAY
4   Easter

APRIL

S	M	T	W	T	F	S
				1	2	3
4	5	6	7	8	9	10
11	12	13	14	15	16	17
18	19	20	21	22	23	24
25	26	27	28	29	30	

COLOR MY WORLD

by Diane Evans, Schenectady, NY, 55" x 55". This original design evolved from an exercise in drawing a motif on 1/8 of a folded piece of paper and reflecting that motif eight times. A winner of several awards in Innovative Appliqué categories including Road to California, Ontario, CA; National Quilt Extravaganza, Harrisburg, PA; and A World of Quilts, Manchester, NH. Juried into AQS Quilt Expo, Des Moines, IA.

April

MONDAY
5

TUESDAY
6

WEDNESDAY
7

THURSDAY
8

FRIDAY
9

SATURDAY
10

SUNDAY
11

APRIL

S	M	T	W	T	F	S
				1	2	3
4	5	6	7	8	9	10
11	12	13	14	15	16	17
18	19	20	21	22	23	24
25	26	27	28	29	30	

AQUARIUS

by Rebecca L. Smith, Hermosa, SD, 79" x 72". The original layout and coloration were influenced by Ann Petersen's Fine Feathered Fancy pattern in *Quilters Newsletter*. The quilt is machine pieced and longarm quilted. Displayed at Black Hills Quilt Show, Rapid City, SD.

Features Fine Feathered Fancy pattern by Ann Petersen from *Quilters Newsletter*.

April

MONDAY
12

TUESDAY
13

WEDNESDAY
14

THURSDAY
15

FRIDAY
16

SATURDAY
17

SUNDAY
18

APRIL

S	M	T	W	T	F	S
				1	2	3
4	5	6	7	8	9	10
11	12	13	14	15	16	17
18	19	20	21	22	23	24
25	26	27	28	29	30	

SPRING RIOT

by Mary Ramsey Keasler, Cleveland, TN, 43" x 54". A guild challenge inspired Mary's original design with criteria including using a season of the year and new techniques never attempted. Machine appliquéd, pieced, and quilted with trapunto and free-motion embroidery. Featured at Museum Center at 5ive Point, Cleveland, TN; McMinn County Heritage Museum Quilt Show (Best Use of Color & Design); and ribbon winner at Smoky Mountain Quilt Show, Knoxville, TN.

April

MONDAY
19

TUESDAY
20

WEDNESDAY
21 — AQS Quilt Show & Contest

THURSDAY
22 — AQS Quilt Show & Contest

FRIDAY
23 — AQS Quilt Show & Contest

SATURDAY
24 — AQS Quilt Show & Contest

SUNDAY
25

APRIL

S	M	T	W	T	F	S
				1	2	3
4	5	6	7	8	9	10
11	12	13	14	15	16	17
18	19	20	21	22	23	24
25	26	27	28	29	30	

JACOBEAN PINEAPPLE STAR

by Kathleen Moorhead Johnson, Alexander, ND, 81" x 81". Inspired by patterns from Sharon Rexroad and Patricia Campbell, Kathleen hand appliquéd the corner and edge blocks to complement the paper-pieced pineapple star. A triple-ribbon winner at Indian Summer Show, Fargo, ND; and Judges' Choice at Minnesota State Quilt Show in Rochester.

Features patterns from Sharon Rexroad's *Pineapple Stars: Sparkling Quilts, Perfectly Pieced*, 2005; and designs from *Jacobean Rhapsodies* by Patricia B. Campbell and Mimi Ayars, 1998, C&T Publishing.

April/May

MONDAY
26

TUESDAY
27

WEDNESDAY
28

THURSDAY
29

FRIDAY
30

SATURDAY
1

SUNDAY
2

MAY

S	M	T	W	T	F	S
						1
2	3	4	5	6	7	8
9	10	11	12	13	14	15
16	17	18	19	20	21	22
23	24	25	26	27	28	29
30	31					

SYLVAN SPLASH

by Susan Jackan, Madison, WI, 66" x 67". Inspired by walking in nearby woods with camera in hand, Susan accentuates the serenity and treasure of nature. Foliage originated from real leaves; the background was sponge painted. Machine appliquéd and quilted. First-place winner at Prairie Heritage Quilt Show, Sun Prairie, WI; and displayed at AQS Quilt Show & Contest, Paducah, KY.

May

MONDAY
3

TUESDAY
4

WEDNESDAY
5

THURSDAY
6

FRIDAY
7

SATURDAY
8

SUNDAY
9
Mother's Day

MAY

S	M	T	W	T	F	S
						1
2	3	4	5	6	7	8
9	10	11	12	13	14	15
16	17	18	19	20	21	22
23	24	25	26	27	28	29
30	31					

A HINT OF NORWAY

by Linda Syverson Guild, Bethesda, MD, 36" x 36". This original Rosemaling design was made in fabric to honor Linda's Norwegian grandmother. Features machine and hand appliqué, hand-couched cording, and trapunto. Honorable mention winner: From the Mill Quilt Challenge, Lowell, MA; and NQA Quilt Show, Columbus, OH.

May

MONDAY
10

TUESDAY
11

WEDNESDAY
12

THURSDAY
13

FRIDAY
14

SATURDAY
15

SUNDAY
16

MAY

S	M	T	W	T	F	S
						1
2	3	4	5	6	7	8
9	10	11	12	13	14	15
16	17	18	19	20	21	22
23	24	25	26	27	28	29
30	31					

ALTHEA'S WALTZ IN THE STARLIGHT BALLROOM

by Judith Heyward, Mt. Pleasant, SC, 72" x 72". This original design of flowers dancing around the center is highlighted by crystals to symbolize the reflections from a dancing ball. Fused appliqué with machine stitching and machine quilting. First-place awards at Asheville Quilt Show, NC; Cobblestone Quilt Show, SC; and best machine quilting, Vermont Quilt Festival, Essex Junction.

May

MONDAY
17

TUESDAY
18

WEDNESDAY
19

THURSDAY
20

FRIDAY
21

SATURDAY
22

SUNDAY
23

MAY

S	M	T	W	T	F	S
						1
2	3	4	5	6	7	8
9	10	11	12	13	14	15
16	17	18	19	20	21	22
23	24	25	26	27	28	29
30	31					

GOOD MORNING

by Rosalie Baker, Davenport, IA, 45" x 45". Motivated by the morning glories and mourning doves that Rosalie saw on her deck in the spring and summer, she created this original design. It is both machine and hand appliquéd, machine quilted, and embellished with beads. Juried into AQS Quilt Expo, Des Moines, IA.

May

MONDAY
24

TUESDAY
25

WEDNESDAY
26

THURSDAY
27

FRIDAY
28

SATURDAY
29

SUNDAY
30

MAY

S	M	T	W	T	F	S
						1
2	3	4	5	6	7	8
9	10	11	12	13	14	15
16	17	18	19	20	21	22
23	24	25	26	27	28	29
30	31					

SHINE ON

by Carol J. Cranston, Elkhorn, NE, 85" x 85". Created using the Hawaiian Star pattern by Judy Niemeyer. Quilting this piece of many facets provided Carol with the opportunity to express her joy in using favorite colors. Machine paper pieced. Longarm quilted by Heidi Herring. Juried into AQS Quilt Show & Contest, Paducah, KY.

Features Hawaiian Star pattern by Judy Niemeyer Quilting, ©2005.

May/ June

MONDAY · *Memorial Day*
31

TUESDAY
1

WEDNESDAY
2

THURSDAY
3

FRIDAY
4

SATURDAY
5

SUNDAY
6

JUNE

S	M	T	W	T	F	S
		1	2	3	4	5
6	7	8	9	10	11	12
13	14	15	16	17	18	19
20	21	22	23	24	25	26
27	28	29	30			

LAS FLORES

by Pat Rollie, Los Angeles, CA, 65" x 95". Begun as a one-flower design from a Prismatic Flower class by Barbara Olsen, it became the springboard to create other flowers for the arrangement. Leaves are raw-edge appliquéd with free-motion quilting in various color threads. Viewers' Choice and first-place winner at Glendale Quilt Show, CA; and juried into AQS Quilt Show & Contest, Paducah, KY.

June

MONDAY
7

TUESDAY
8

WEDNESDAY
9

THURSDAY
10

FRIDAY
11

SATURDAY
12

SUNDAY
13

			JUNE			
S	M	T	W	T	F	S
		1	2	3	4	5
6	7	8	9	10	11	12
13	14	15	16	17	18	19
20	21	22	23	24	25	26
27	28	29	30			

THE ANNIVERSARY QUILT

by Margo J. Clabo, Cleveland, TN, 60" x 73". Adapted from Dinah Jeffries' Out of the Baltimore Box patterns from Garden City Gateworks for a 40th anniversary reflecting children, grandchildren, and current home. Hand needleturn appliqué, longarm quilted by Kathy Drew. Displayed at Smoky Mountain Quilt Show, Knoxville, TN; and AQS Quilt Expo, Nashville, TN.

Features Out of the Baltimore Box pattern by Dinah Jeffries, Garden City Gateworks ©1998.

June

MONDAY
14

TUESDAY
15

WEDNESDAY
16

THURSDAY
17

FRIDAY
18

SATURDAY
19

SUNDAY
20

Father's Day

JUNE

S	M	T	W	T	F	S
		1	2	3	4	5
6	7	8	9	10	11	12
13	14	15	16	17	18	19
20	21	22	23	24	25	26
27	28	29	30			

POPPY FIELDS

by Penny Allen, Tucson, AZ, 55" x 55". A picture of a field of California poppies with a clear blue sky was inspiration for this quilt. Penny hand-dyed the fabric for machine appliqué, pieceliqué, and machine quilting. Awards include Judges' Choice at Quilt Fiesta, Tucson, AZ; and ribbon winner at Home Machine Quilter Showcase, Salt Lake City, UT.

Appliqué designs used in quilt: Poppy (blocks) & an adaptation of Clump of Poppies (border & center block) by Susan R. DuLaney, Distinctive Pieces ©1990 & 1991.

June

MONDAY
21

TUESDAY
22

WEDNESDAY
23

THURSDAY
24

FRIDAY
25

SATURDAY
26

SUNDAY
27

JUNE

S	M	T	W	T	F	S
		1	2	3	4	5
6	7	8	9	10	11	12
13	14	15	16	17	18	19
20	21	22	23	24	25	26
27	28	29	30			

SKYROCKET

by Tess Thorsberg, Macon, GA, 77" x 90". From the book *Scrap Frenzy: Even More Quick-Pieced Scrap Quilts* by Sally Schneider, this quilt was made specifically for a wedding using favorite bright color fabrics. Machine pieced and quilted. A winner at the Georgia National Fair, Perry; and juried into the AQS Quilt Show & Contest, Paducah, KY.

Features Skyrocket pattern from *Scrap Frenzy: Even More Quick-Pieced Scrap Quilts* by Sally Schneider, Martingale & Co. ©2001.

June/July

MONDAY
28

TUESDAY
29

WEDNESDAY
30

THURSDAY
1

FRIDAY
2

SATURDAY
3

SUNDAY
4
Independence Day

JULY

S	M	T	W	T	F	S
				1	2	3
4	5	6	7	8	9	10
11	12	13	14	15	16	17
18	19	20	21	22	23	24
25	26	27	28	29	30	31

PLAYING IN THE PARK

by Nancy Sterett Martin, Owensboro, KY, 41" x 47". Several photographs and drawings were combined in creating this quilt. Photo-transfer techniques were used for the leaves; the girls' features and clothing were hand painted. Machine quilted. Juried into AQS Quilt Show & Contest, Paducah, KY.

July

MONDAY
5

TUESDAY
6

WEDNESDAY
7

THURSDAY
8

FRIDAY
9

SATURDAY
10

SUNDAY
11

JULY

S	M	T	W	T	F	S
				1	2	3
4	5	6	7	8	9	10
11	12	13	14	15	16	17
18	19	20	21	22	23	24
25	26	27	28	29	30	31

WILDFLOWER MEDLEY III

by Carol Nartowicz, Rutland, VT, 86" x 86". The pattern used for inspiration was Flowers & Stems, from Bea Oglesby's *Wildflower Album*. Carol enjoyed the freezer-paper method of appliqué and radiating lines. Ribbon winner at Vermont Quilt Festival, Essex Junction; and juried into AQS Quilt Expo, Nashville, TN.

Features Flowers & Stems from *Wildflower Album* by Bea Oglesby, AQS ©1998.

Start the new decade with...
QUILT ART 2011

A tradition at AQS, this calendar greets you each week with a new and beautiful quilt. The sturdy spiral binding keeps it lying flat on your desk. There's plenty of space for jotting down appointments, accomplishments, or just random thoughts.

#8011, 7" x 9", 112 pages $13.95

Quilt Art 2011 Engagement Calendar available April 15, 2010

ORDER TOLL FREE
7:00 a.m. through 5:00 p.m. CST
1-800-626-5420

— — — — — — — Detach and Return — — — — — — —

| | #8011 | Quilt Art 2011 Engagement Calendar | @ $13.95 | |
| | #7800 | Quilt Art 2010 Engagement Calendar | @ $13.95 | |

For more information on becoming a member of AQS, check here ❏ **#2323**

*Postage & Handling
KY residents add 6% sales tax
TOTAL ENCLOSED

Method of Payment
Make checks payable to American Quilter's Society.
I have enclosed a check for $_____ Ck#_____

Charge my: ❏ MasterCard ❏ VISA ❏ DISCOVER/NOVUS Exp._____
Card # ☐☐☐☐ ☐☐☐☐ ☐☐☐☐ ☐☐☐☐
Signature_____

Name_____
Address_____
City_____ State_____ Zip_____
Country_____

POLICY — One-day "Sudden Service." Postage and handling, U.S. customers, $5.00 for first book and 60¢ for each additional book. Canadian/international shipping charges: 10-15 business day delivery, $11.00 postage per book. No open accounts. Send check with order. Canadian customers must pay in U.S. funds only. Kentucky customers without a Kentucky sales tax number must add 6% sales tax. Prices subject to change. Orders shipped the most cost-effective way (most often U.S. Postal Service).

American Quilter's Society
P. O. Box 3290 • Paducah, KY 42002-3290
Phone: 270-898-7903 • FAX: 270-898-1173
www.AmericanQuilter.com

EC1

July

MONDAY
12

TUESDAY
13

WEDNESDAY
14
AQS Quilt Expo, Knoxville

THURSDAY
15
AQS Quilt Expo, Knoxville

FRIDAY
16
AQS Quilt Expo, Knoxville

SATURDAY
17
AQS Quilt Expo, Knoxville

SUNDAY
18

S	M	T	W	T	F	S
				1	2	3
4	5	6	7	8	9	10
11	12	13	14	15	16	17
18	19	20	21	22	23	24
25	26	27	28	29	30	31

JULY

I DREAM OF JEN'S POPPIES

by Debra Ramsey, Lexington, OH, 51" x 52". After dreamy thoughts of big orange poppies, this hand-appliquéd and quilted piece was created. In adapting the Patricia Cox Poppies pattern, Debra used a machine-pieced Trip Around the World background in neutral fabrics to enhance the bold flowers in various shades of orange and green. Exhibited at NQA, Columbus, OH.

Features Poppies pattern by Patricia Cox, One of a Kind Quilting Designs ©1989.

July

MONDAY
19

TUESDAY
20

WEDNESDAY
21

THURSDAY
22

FRIDAY
23

SATURDAY
24

SUNDAY
25

JULY

S	M	T	W	T	F	S
				1	2	3
4	5	6	7	8	9	10
11	12	13	14	15	16	17
18	19	20	21	22	23	24
25	26	27	28	29	30	31

CIRCLE THE WAGONS

by Kathy Lichtendahl, Clark, WY, 46" x 46". Paper piecing eased the challenge of making the wagon wheels appear round. Each of the pioneer women is dressed differently with their aprons reflecting old patchwork designs. The original design won a first-place award at Quilter's Rendezvous, Rock Springs, WY. Also shown at Yellowstone Quilt Fest, Cody, WY; and International Quilt Festival, Houston, TX.

July/August

MONDAY
26

TUESDAY
27

WEDNESDAY
28

THURSDAY
29

FRIDAY
30

SATURDAY
31

SUNDAY
1

AUGUST

S	M	T	W	T	F	S
1	2	3	4	5	6	7
8	9	10	11	12	13	14
15	16	17	18	19	20	21
22	23	24	25	26	27	28
29	30	31				

FORTY YEARS AND FOREVER

by Suzanne Bishop, Tucson, AZ, 31" x 36". A photo of Suzanne's husband, Towne, while camping in Colorado, was the inspiration for this quilt. Creating depth in the forest and details in the foreground was the most challenging. Use of embellishments, trapunto, and machine quilting with the appli-bond technique enhanced the outcome of this piece. First-place winner at Quilt Fiesta! in Tucson, AZ.

August

MONDAY
2

TUESDAY
3

WEDNESDAY
4

THURSDAY
5

FRIDAY
6

SATURDAY
7

SUNDAY
8

AUGUST

S	M	T	W	T	F	S
1	2	3	4	5	6	7
8	9	10	11	12	13	14
15	16	17	18	19	20	21
22	23	24	25	26	27	28
29	30	31				

LOTUS BLOSSOM

by Alice Means, Bolton, CT, 60" x 64". Layered cutting gave Alice multiple repeats to establish the design from *Serendipity Quilts* by Sara Nephew. Machine embroidered and quilted. Ribbon winner at Maine Quilts, Augusta; and juried into AQS Quilt Expo, Des Moines, IA.

Features Lotus Flower or Dancing Lotus from *Serendipity Quilts*, Sara Nephew/Clearview Triangles, an import of Alicia's Attic Inc. ©2004.

August

MONDAY
9

TUESDAY
10

WEDNESDAY
11   Ramadan

THURSDAY
12

FRIDAY
13

SATURDAY
14

SUNDAY
15

AUGUST

S	M	T	W	T	F	S
1	2	3	4	5	6	7
8	9	10	11	12	13	14
15	16	17	18	19	20	21
22	23	24	25	26	27	28
29	30	31				

ON A STORMY, CLOUDY, DAY
by Diane Smith, Merritt Island, FL, 34" x 43". A photo of a fruit stand was the inspiration for this quilt, featuring Diane's hand-dyed fabrics and "organic edges." Machine pieced and quilted with a walking foot on a home sewing machine.

August

MONDAY
16

TUESDAY
17

WEDNESDAY
18

THURSDAY
19

FRIDAY
20

SATURDAY
21

SUNDAY
22

AUGUST

S	M	T	W	T	F	S
1	2	3	4	5	6	7
8	9	10	11	12	13	14
15	16	17	18	19	20	21
22	23	24	25	26	27	28
29	30	31				

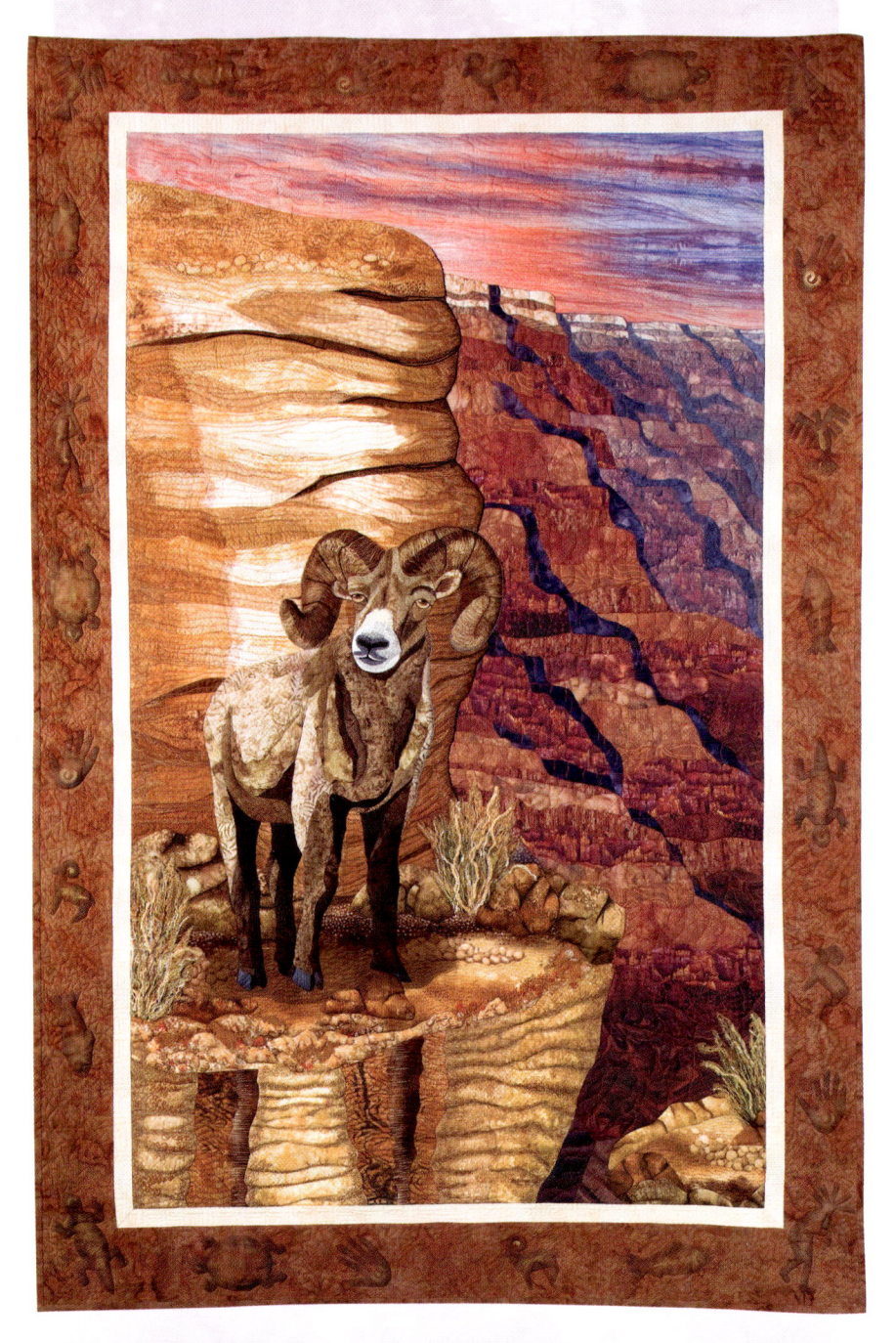

GRAND CANYON MONARCH

by Donna Cherry, Bend, OR, 42" x 63". The original design comes from Donna's love of nature and the opportunity to explore textiles as a fine art medium. Most Outstanding Art Quilt winner at Road to California, Ontario, CA; juried into Pacific Northwest Quilt Fest, Seattle, WA; and AQS Quilt Show & Contest, Paducah, KY.

August

MONDAY
23

TUESDAY
24

WEDNESDAY
25

THURSDAY
26

FRIDAY
27

SATURDAY
28

SUNDAY
29

AUGUST

S	M	T	W	T	F	S
1	2	3	4	5	6	7
8	9	10	11	12	13	14
15	16	17	18	19	20	21
22	23	24	25	26	27	28
29	30	31				

STATIC CHAOS

by Patricia Delaney, Abington, MA, 65" x 74". This scrap quilt, based on Karen Stone's Indian Orange Peel pattern, uses almost no duplicate fabrics. Machine pieced, quilted, and embroidered with each scalloped edge finished with handmade piping and embellished handmade polymer clay buttons. Best Color winner at Mid-Atlantic Quilt Fest and Best Piecing award at Vermont Quilt Festival, Essex Junction.

Features Indian Orange Peel pattern by Karen K. Stone ©1994.

August/September

MONDAY
30

TUESDAY
31

WEDNESDAY
1

THURSDAY
2

FRIDAY
3

SATURDAY
4

SUNDAY
5

SEPTEMBER

S	M	T	W	T	F	S
			1	2	3	4
5	6	7	8	9	10	11
12	13	14	15	16	17	18
19	20	21	22	23	24	25
26	27	28	29	30		

A LITTLE DAB'LL DO YA

by Ellen Kalilel Robinson, Germantown, MD, 34" x 33". The original design was based on a photo of Ellen's husband, a watercolorist, who inspired the theme for her Gaithersburg, MD, guild challenge — A Chip Off the Old Paint Bucket. Juried into AQS Quilt Expo, Nashville, TN.

September

MONDAY
6
Labor Day

TUESDAY
7

WEDNESDAY
8

THURSDAY
9
Rosh Hashanah

FRIDAY
10

SATURDAY
11

SUNDAY
12

SEPTEMBER

S	M	T	W	T	F	S
			1	2	3	4
5	6	7	8	9	10	11
12	13	14	15	16	17	18
19	20	21	22	23	24	25
26	27	28	29	30		

MY NOBLE EAGLE

by Darlene Christopherson, China Spring, TX, 67" x 67". On September 11, 2001, Darlene began drawing this original eagle and choosing fabrics for her quilt. A hand-pieced traditional Lone Star surrounds the hand-appliquéd eagle. Machine quilted and named after the military effort following 9-11. Shown at International Quilt Festival, Houston, TX.

September

MONDAY
13

TUESDAY
14

WEDNESDAY
15

THURSDAY
16

FRIDAY
17

SATURDAY　　*Yom Kippur*
18

SUNDAY
19

			SEPTEMBER			
S	M	T	W	T	F	S
			1	2	3	4
5	6	7	8	9	10	11
12	13	14	15	16	17	18
19	20	21	22	23	24	25
26	27	28	29	30		

LETTERS FROM A BROAD

by Janet Stone, Overland Park, KS, 31" x 76". Inspired by a love of alphabet, batik fabrics, and an extensive collection of embellishments, the original design came quickly on a napkin at lunchtime. Machine pieced and quilted; all embellishments were sewn on by hand. Double ribbon winner at Minnesota Quilters' Show in Rochester; Honorable Mention at AQS Quilt Expo, Des Moines, IA.

September

MONDAY
20

TUESDAY
21

WEDNESDAY
22

THURSDAY
23

FRIDAY
24

SATURDAY
25

SUNDAY
26

SEPTEMBER

S	M	T	W	T	F	S
			1	2	3	4
5	6	7	8	9	10	11
12	13	14	15	16	17	18
19	20	21	22	23	24	25
26	27	28	29	30		

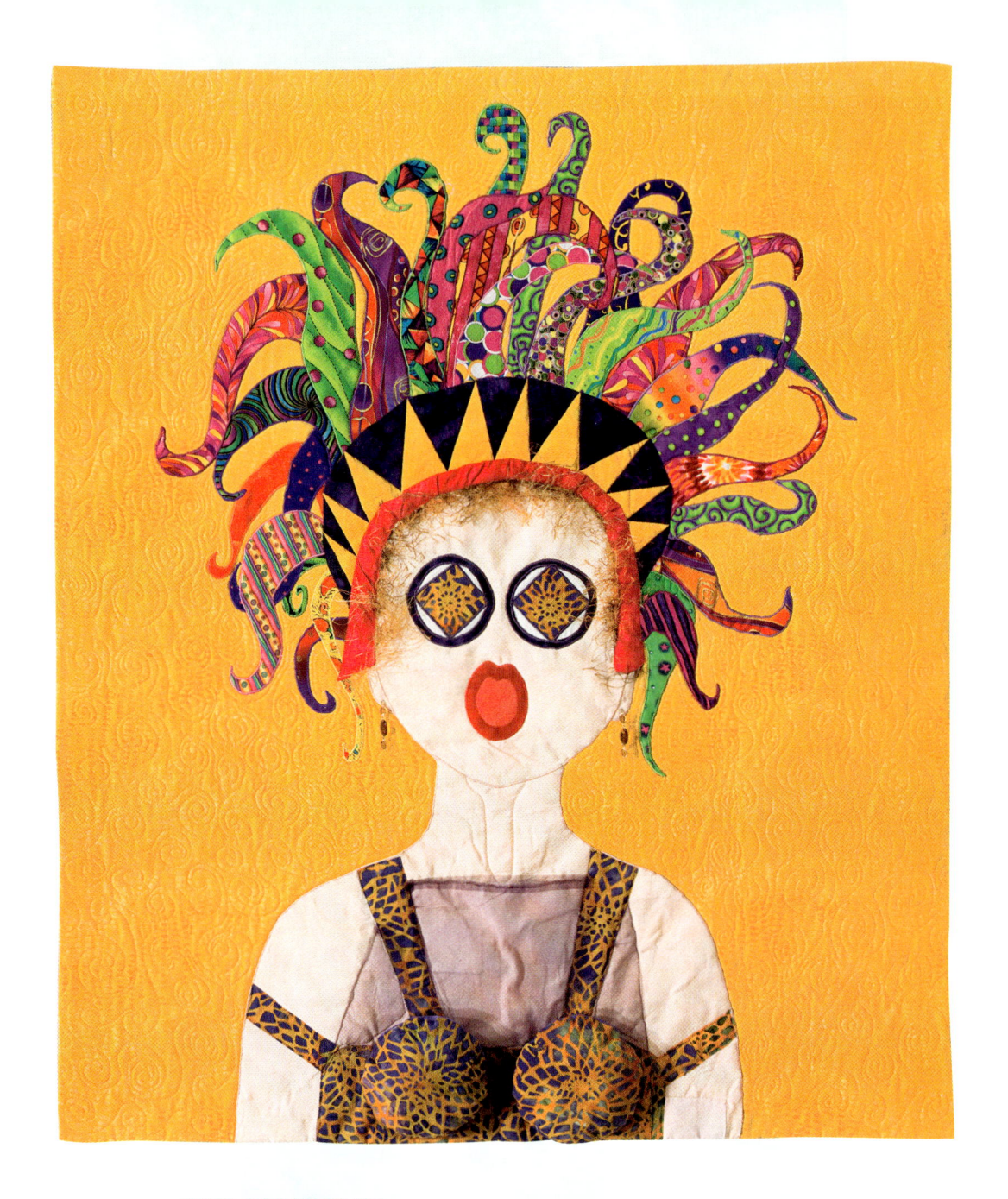

BAD HAIR DAY

by Judy M. Shelton, Boynton Beach, FL, 34" x 40". Inspired by the guild challenge Going to Pieces, the original design combines Medusa and *The Scream* by Edvard Munch. Ribbon winner in Gold Coast Quilter's Challenge, Boca Raton, FL; juried into AQS Quilt Expo, Nashville, TN.

September/October

MONDAY
27

TUESDAY
28

WEDNESDAY
29

THURSDAY
30

FRIDAY
1

SATURDAY
2

SUNDAY
3

OCTOBER

S	M	T	W	T	F	S
					1	2
3	4	5	6	7	8	9
10	11	12	13	14	15	16
17	18	19	20	21	22	23
24	25	26	27	28	29	30
31						

EASTERN WINDS

by Ravoe Nelson, Pensacola, FL, 93" x 93". The Mariner's Compass-inspired design with encircled star and starbursts is named for the hurricanes that hit the Gulf Coast. Machine pieced and machine quilted on a home sewing machine. Awarded the Viewers' Choice ribbon at Pensacola Quilter's Guild Show.

October

MONDAY
4

TUESDAY
5

WEDNESDAY
6
AQS Quilt Show & Contest

THURSDAY
7
AQS Quilt Show & Contest

FRIDAY
8
AQS Quilt Show & Contest

SATURDAY
9
AQS Quilt Show & Contest

SUNDAY
10

OCTOBER

S	M	T	W	T	F	S
					1	2
3	4	5	6	7	8	9
10	11	12	13	14	15	16
17	18	19	20	21	22	23
24	25	26	27	28	29	30
31						

I LOVE FALL

by Nancy E. Colladay, Kensington, MD, 36" x 41". Inspired by a Clip Art design, Nancy used an old pair of jeans and real leather for the hat to bring this scarecrow to life. Techniques included stenciling the pumpkins and leaves, raw-edge machine appliqué, and machine quilting. Displayed at Friendship Star Quilters Show, Gaithersburg, MD; and juried into AQS Quilt Expo, Nashville, TN.

October

MONDAY   *Columbus Day*
11

TUESDAY
12

WEDNESDAY
13

THURSDAY
14

FRIDAY
15

SATURDAY
16

SUNDAY
17

OCTOBER

S	M	T	W	T	F	S
					1	2
3	4	5	6	7	8	9
10	11	12	13	14	15	16
17	18	19	20	21	22	23
24	25	26	27	28	29	30
31						

SOUTHWESTERN STAR

by Kathryn Sims, Alexis, IL, 96" x 96". A class with Donna Lanmen and the 8 Red Birds pattern by Lorene Liberty-Curtis prompted Kathryn's first project after retirement, her first Lone Star, and her first attempt at hand appliqué. Machine pieced and quilted. Best of Show at Mississippi Valley Show, Davenport, IA; ribbon winner at NQA in Columbus, OH; and juried into AQS Quilt Show & Contest, Paducah, KY.

Features 8 Red Birds pattern by Lorene Liberty-Curtis, Liberty Quilters.

October

MONDAY
18

TUESDAY
19

WEDNESDAY
20

THURSDAY
21

FRIDAY
22

SATURDAY
23

SUNDAY
24

OCTOBER

S	M	T	W	T	F	S
					1	2
3	4	5	6	7	8	9
10	11	12	13	14	15	16
17	18	19	20	21	22	23
24	25	26	27	28	29	30
31						

PUMPKIN PATCH

by Laurie Tigner, Rapid City, SD, 68" x 84". After quilting for only a year, this original design was created of memories, imagination, and lots of sketches. The witch's pose came from a photo of Laurie's daughter eating candy out of a plastic pumpkin. Machine appliquéd and quilted. A ribbon winner at Black Hills Quilt Show, Rapid City, SD.

October

MONDAY
25

TUESDAY
26

WEDNESDAY
27

THURSDAY
28

FRIDAY
29

SATURDAY
30

SUNDAY
31

Halloween

OCTOBER

S	M	T	W	T	F	S
					1	2
3	4	5	6	7	8	9
10	11	12	13	14	15	16
17	18	19	20	21	22	23
24	25	26	27	28	29	30
31						

LOOK WHAT I DID TO MAMA'S DRAPES

by Julee Prose, Ottumwa, IA, 86" x 92". Julee hand appliquéd and quilted the diagonal grid to fill in the background, with freehand designs on the large print borders. This original quilt was a winner at Minnesota Quilt Show, Rochester, and the Minnesota State Fair. Shown at Road to California, Ontario, CA; and Des Moines Area Quilt Guild Show at the AQS Quilt Expo, Des Moines, IA.

November

MONDAY
1

TUESDAY
2

WEDNESDAY
3

THURSDAY
4

FRIDAY
5

SATURDAY
6

SUNDAY
7

Daylight Saving Time ends

			NOVEMBER			
S	M	T	W	T	F	S
	1	2	3	4	5	6
7	8	9	10	11	12	13
14	15	16	17	18	19	20
21	22	23	24	25	26	27
28	29	30				

CATCHING THE BREEZE

by Janet Bergeron, Norwalk, IA, 29" x 37". Old windmills along the roadways have always fascinated Janet. She decided to capture this architectural view with sun reflections and shadows in her original design quilt. It was included in the Iowa State Fair Fine Arts Division and at the Des Moines Area Quilt Guild Show at the AQS Quilt Expo, Des Moines, IA.

November

MONDAY
8

TUESDAY
9

WEDNESDAY
10

THURSDAY
11
Veterans Day

FRIDAY
12

SATURDAY
13

SUNDAY
14

NOVEMBER

S	M	T	W	T	F	S
	1	2	3	4	5	6
7	8	9	10	11	12	13
14	15	16	17	18	19	20
21	22	23	24	25	26	27
28	29	30				

...AND SOMETIMES Y

by Julie A. Sefton, Bartlett, TN, 51" x 51". These free-pieced vowels laugh and play between their happy and colorful borders in an original design. Machine quilted by Christine Ballard. Juried into AQS Quilt Expo, Nashville, TN.

November

MONDAY
15

TUESDAY
16

WEDNESDAY
17

THURSDAY
18

FRIDAY
19

SATURDAY
20

SUNDAY
21

NOVEMBER

S	M	T	W	T	F	S
	1	2	3	4	5	6
7	8	9	10	11	12	13
14	15	16	17	18	19	20
21	22	23	24	25	26	27
28	29	30				

MIDNIGHT IN PARADISE

by Friendship Knot Quilters' Guild, Bradenton, FL, 91" x 91". Two Judy Niemeyer patterns, Bird of Paradise and Tropical Flowers, were used by guild members to create this large quilt. Machine pieced and appliquéd. Longarm quilted by Marie Snyder. A ribbon winner at National Quilting Association Show in Columbus, OH; and juried into AQS Quilt Expo, Nashville, TN.

Features Tropical Flowers and Bird of Paradise patterns by Judy Niemeyer Quilting ©2002 & 2004.

November

MONDAY
22

TUESDAY
23

WEDNESDAY
24

THURSDAY   *Thanksgiving*
25

FRIDAY
26

SATURDAY
27

SUNDAY
28

NOVEMBER

S	M	T	W	T	F	S
	1	2	3	4	5	6
7	8	9	10	11	12	13
14	15	16	17	18	19	20
21	22	23	24	25	26	27
28	29	30				

DON'T GO OFF THE BEATEN PATH

by Patricia Kersch, Reddick, IL, 40" x 40". A snapshot from a vacation to Siena, Italy, inspired this landscape. Patricia watched the street scene come to life after adding each building and often wondering what was at the end of this road. Machine quilted. Juried into AQS Quilt Expo, Nashville, TN.

November/December

MONDAY
29

TUESDAY
30

WEDNESDAY
1

THURSDAY Hanukkah
2

FRIDAY
3

SATURDAY
4

SUNDAY
5

DECEMBER

S	M	T	W	T	F	S
				1	2	3	4
5	6	7	8	9	10	11
12	13	14	15	16	17	18
19	20	21	22	23	24	25
26	27	28	29	30	31	

MAGICAL MEDALLIONS

by Patty Doarn Goodsell, Arivaca, AZ, 84" x 84". After taking Karen Kay Buckley's class, making one block was just not enough. Using Karen's pattern, a non-traditional batik background, needleturn appliqué, and hand quilting (30 needles to quilt), Patty learned something new with each block. Awarded with five ribbons at the Tucson Quilters Guild, including Best of Show and Viewers' Choice.

Features Magical Medallions pattern by Karen Kay Buckley ©2003.

December

MONDAY
6

TUESDAY
7

WEDNESDAY
8

THURSDAY
9

FRIDAY
10

SATURDAY
11

SUNDAY
12

			DECEMBER			
S	M	T	W	T	F	S
			1	2	3	4
5	6	7	8	9	10	11
12	13	14	15	16	17	18
19	20	21	22	23	24	25
26	27	28	29	30	31	

WARMTH OF THE SUN

by Katalin Shier, Apple Valley, MN, 80" x 80". After the center of the original, hand-drafted design "rested" for six years, the remainder of the quilt was ready within one day at a retreat. The orange daisies were cut freehand with folded fabric. Machine pieced, hand appliquéd, and machine quilted with original quilt designs. Ribbon winner at Minnesota Quilters Show; juried into AQS Quilt Show & Contest, Paducah, KY.

December

MONDAY
13

TUESDAY
14

WEDNESDAY
15

THURSDAY
16

FRIDAY
17

SATURDAY
18

SUNDAY
19

DECEMBER

S	M	T	W	T	F	S
			1	2	3	4
5	6	7	8	9	10	11
12	13	14	15	16	17	18
19	20	21	22	23	24	25
26	27	28	29	30	31	

IT'S CHRISTMAS TIME

by Jeri Saldinger, Oro Valley, AZ, 50" x 50". The Season of Joy pattern by Mary Sorensen features hand appliqué, metallic fabric and thread, and embroidered embellishments. Quilted by Mary Vaneecke. First-place winner at Quilt Fiesta, Tucson, AZ.

Features Season of Joy pattern by Mary Sorensen, Mary Sorensen Design Source, Inc. ©1996.

December

MONDAY
20

TUESDAY
21

WEDNESDAY
22

THURSDAY
23

FRIDAY
24

SATURDAY
25
Christmas

SUNDAY
26
Kwanzaa

DECEMBER

S	M	T	W	T	F	S
			1	2	3	4
5	6	7	8	9	10	11
12	13	14	15	16	17	18
19	20	21	22	23	24	25
26	27	28	29	30	31	

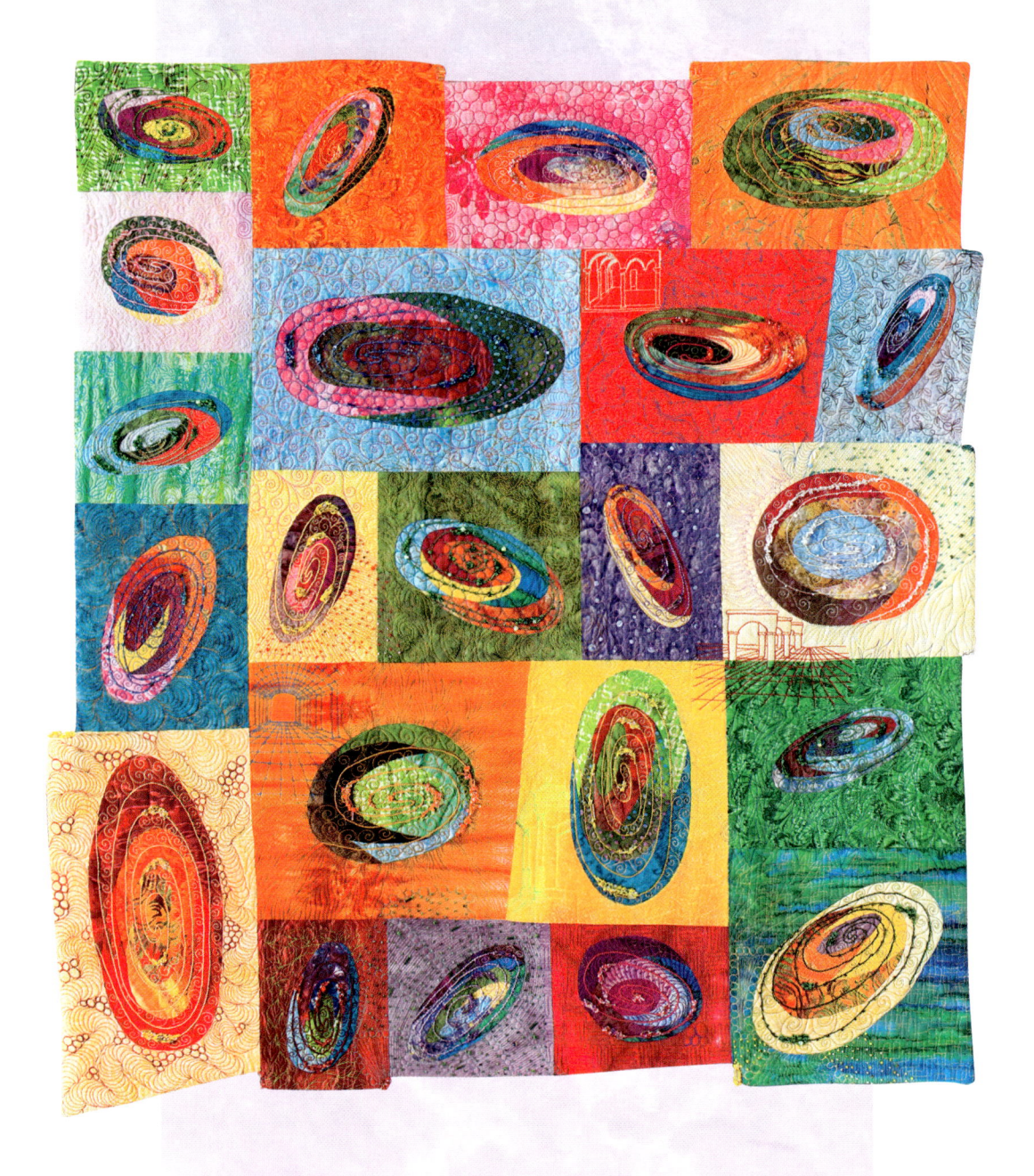

DREAM OF ETERNITY

by Sylvia G. Snyder, Hurlock, MD, 38" x 42". Sylvia used her own invented machine-reverse appliqué technique to construct the 22 blocks. She incorporated bobbin work and hand beading. Freehand machine quilting features architectural designs by her husband, Richard. Ribbon winner at Pennsylvania National Quilt Extravaganza, Harrisburg; and juried into AQS Quilt Expo, Des Moines, IA.

December/January

MONDAY
27

TUESDAY
28

WEDNESDAY
29

THURSDAY
30

FRIDAY
31

SATURDAY
1
New Year's Day

SUNDAY
2

JANUARY

S	M	T	W	T	F	S
						1
2	3	4	5	6	7	8
9	10	11	12	13	14	15
16	17	18	19	20	21	22
23	24	25	26	27	28	29
30	31					

Quilt Art 2010

A year full of fabulous quilts!

Here is a collection of 54 breathtaking, prizewinning quilts from around the country. Klaudeen Hansen, certified judge and national traveling quilt teacher, is an expert at selecting quilts that will amaze and inspire you.

Superb workmanship, exciting fabric selection, original designs, and inventive interpretations of classic patterns abound. You'll be presented with a new quilt each week with just a turn of the page.

Klaudeen Hansen

Use the week-at-a-glance pages to keep you on track while you enjoy the best of today's quilting community.

Editors: Chrystal Abhalter & Andi Reynolds
Designer: Angela Schade

Additional copies of this calendar may be obtained from your favorite bookseller, sewing center, craft shop, or from

American Quilter's Society
PO Box 3290
Paducah, KY 42002-3290
1-800-626-5420 • fax (270) 898-1173
www.AmericanQuilter.com
info@AQSquilt.com

@$13.95 per copy
Add $3.00 to cover postage and handling.

Copyright ©2009 by the American Quilter's Society

All rights reserved. No part of this book may be reproduced, stored in any retrieval system, or transmitted in any form, or by any means including but not limited to electronic, mechanical, photocopy, recording, or otherwise, without the written consent of the publisher.

Proudly printed and bound in the United States of America.

The publisher has made every effort to ensure the accuracy of information in this calendar but cannot assume liability for any errors.

2010

JANUARY
S	M	T	W	T	F	S
					1	2
3	4	5	6	7	8	9
10	11	12	13	14	15	16
17	18	19	20	21	22	23
24	25	26	27	28	29	30
31						

FEBRUARY
S	M	T	W	T	F	S
	1	2	3	4	5	6
7	8	9	10	11	12	13
14	15	16	17	18	19	20
21	22	23	24	25	26	27
28						

MARCH
S	M	T	W	T	F	S
	1	2	3	4	5	6
7	8	9	10	11	12	13
14	15	16	17	18	19	20
21	22	23	24	25	26	27
28	29	30	31			

APRIL
S	M	T	W	T	F	S
				1	2	3
4	5	6	7	8	9	10
11	12	13	14	15	16	17
18	19	20	21	22	23	24
25	26	27	28	29	30	

MAY
S	M	T	W	T	F	S
						1
2	3	4	5	6	7	8
9	10	11	12	13	14	15
16	17	18	19	20	21	22
23	24	25	26	27	28	29
30	31					

JUNE
S	M	T	W	T	F	S
		1	2	3	4	5
6	7	8	9	10	11	12
13	14	15	16	17	18	19
20	21	22	23	24	25	26
27	28	29	30			

JULY
S	M	T	W	T	F	S
				1	2	3
4	5	6	7	8	9	10
11	12	13	14	15	16	17
18	19	20	21	22	23	24
25	26	27	28	29	30	31

AUGUST
S	M	T	W	T	F	S
1	2	3	4	5	6	7
8	9	10	11	12	13	14
15	16	17	18	19	20	21
22	23	24	25	26	27	28
29	30	31				

SEPTEMBER
S	M	T	W	T	F	S
			1	2	3	4
5	6	7	8	9	10	11
12	13	14	15	16	17	18
19	20	21	22	23	24	25
26	27	28	29	30		

OCTOBER
S	M	T	W	T	F	S
					1	2
3	4	5	6	7	8	9
10	11	12	13	14	15	16
17	18	19	20	21	22	23
24	25	26	27	28	29	30
31						

NOVEMBER
S	M	T	W	T	F	S
	1	2	3	4	5	6
7	8	9	10	11	12	13
14	15	16	17	18	19	20
21	22	23	24	25	26	27
28	29	30				

DECEMBER
S	M	T	W	T	F	S
			1	2	3	4
5	6	7	8	9	10	11
12	13	14	15	16	17	18
19	20	21	22	23	24	25
26	27	28	29	30	31	

2011

JANUARY
S	M	T	W	T	F	S
						1
2	3	4	5	6	7	8
9	10	11	12	13	14	15
16	17	18	19	20	21	22
23	24	25	26	27	28	29
30	31					

FEBRUARY
S	M	T	W	T	F	S
		1	2	3	4	5
6	7	8	9	10	11	12
13	14	15	16	17	18	19
20	21	22	23	24	25	26
27	28					

MARCH
S	M	T	W	T	F	S
		1	2	3	4	5
6	7	8	9	10	11	12
13	14	15	16	17	18	19
20	21	22	23	24	25	26
27	28	29	30	31		

APRIL
S	M	T	W	T	F	S
					1	2
3	4	5	6	7	8	9
10	11	12	13	14	15	16
17	18	19	20	21	22	23
24	25	26	27	28	29	30

MAY
S	M	T	W	T	F	S
1	2	3	4	5	6	7
8	9	10	11	12	13	14
15	16	17	18	19	20	21
22	23	24	25	26	27	28
29	30	31				

JUNE
S	M	T	W	T	F	S
			1	2	3	4
5	6	7	8	9	10	11
12	13	14	15	16	17	18
19	20	21	22	23	24	25
26	27	28	29	30		

JULY
S	M	T	W	T	F	S
					1	2
3	4	5	6	7	8	9
10	11	12	13	14	15	16
17	18	19	20	21	22	23
24	25	26	27	28	29	30
31						

AUGUST
S	M	T	W	T	F	S
	1	2	3	4	5	6
7	8	9	10	11	12	13
14	15	16	17	18	19	20
21	22	23	24	25	26	27
28	29	30	31			

SEPTEMBER
S	M	T	W	T	F	S
				1	2	3
4	5	6	7	8	9	10
11	12	13	14	15	16	17
18	19	20	21	22	23	24
25	26	27	28	29	30	

OCTOBER
S	M	T	W	T	F	S
						1
2	3	4	5	6	7	8
9	10	11	12	13	14	15
16	17	18	19	20	21	22
23	24	25	26	27	28	29
30	31					

NOVEMBER
S	M	T	W	T	F	S
		1	2	3	4	5
6	7	8	9	10	11	12
13	14	15	16	17	18	19
20	21	22	23	24	25	26
27	28	29	30			

DECEMBER
S	M	T	W	T	F	S
				1	2	3
4	5	6	7	8	9	10
11	12	13	14	15	16	17
18	19	20	21	22	23	24
25	26	27	28	29	30	31

Notes